Supernatural Love

Alan Leonhardt

Copyright © 2021 by Alan F. Leonhardt

All Rights Reserved. No part of this publication may be reproduced, stored in a retrieval system, or transmitted in any form or by any means - for example, electronic, photocopy, and recording - without the prior written permission of the publisher. The only exception is brief quotations in printed reviews.

Published by Lionheart Publications,
  a division of Lionheart Ministries
1600 W. State Rd
Hastings, MI 49058
alanleonhardt@gmail.com

Unless otherwise indicated, scripture quotations are taken from the New King James Version. Copyright © 1982 Thomas Nelson, Inc. Used by permission. All rights reserved.

Scripture quotations marked NIV are taken from the Holy Bible, New International Version Copyright © 1973, 1978, 1984 by International Bible Society. Used by permission of Zondervan. All rights reserved.

Scripture quotations marked AMP are taken from the Amplified Bible. Copyright © 1954, 1958, 1962, 1964, 1965, 1987 by the Lockman Foundation. Used by permission.

Cover design, editing, and interior design by Kathy Mayo

ISBNs: 978-1-7348354-6-5 (printed)
       978-1-7348354-7-2 (ebook)

First edition: October, 2021
Printed in the United States of America

Contents

Introduction 7

SECTION 1 ~ The Love of God

Day 1
God's Love is the Foundation 10

Day 2
God is Love 13

Day 3
There is No Fear in Love. 16

Day 4
The Compassion of God 18

Day 5
God is Good. 21

Day 6
The Passion 24

Day 7
The Parable of the Good Samaritan 27

SECTION 2 ~ Accessing God's Love

Day 8
Courageous Love 31

Day 9
Love is Not Easily Offended 34

Day 10
Love Fulfills the Law 37

Day 11
The Spirit of Love..................................40

Day 12
Leaving Your First Love..........................43

Day 13
Pray in the Holy Spirit...........................47

Day 14
Mercy and Truth...................................50

SECTION 3 ~ Tough Love

Day 15
Loving Discipline..................................54

Day 16
As Many as I Love, I Rebuke....................57

Day 17
Don't Be Unequally Yoked......................60

Day 18
Love is Discerning.................................63

Day 19
Romantic Love.....................................66

Day 20
Love and Marriage................................70

Day 21
Love One Another.................................73

Epilogue..77

Previous Books by Alan Leonhardt

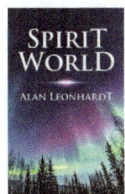

Spirit World, 2019

There is a deep spiritual side to the Christian experience.
In this book, Dr Leonhardt relates his own
personal journey with dreams, visions,
hearing from God, speaking in tongues,
and other powerful gifts of the Holy Spirit.

Pathway to Promotion, 2020

God has a destiny for every believer. He wants to bless you
exceedingly, abundantly and above your wildest dreams.
As we cooperate with God's principles for advancement,
we will break out of a mediocre Christian life
and find the Pathway to Promotion.

Supernatural Joy, 2020

How is your joy level? Jesus said, "Ask that your Joy may be full"
(John 16:24). In this 21-day devotional,
you will learn how to access the "Supernatural Joy"
of God. Learn what it means to hope and have
a positive expectation of your future.

Supernatural Peace, 2021

What would you give for some peace of mind and spirit?
The Bible promises a "Supernatural Peace" that passes
all understanding to the followers of Jesus.

In this 21-day Devotional, you will cultivate the fruit
of peace in your life. These timeless truths will
deepen your faith and bring stability to your soul.

Dedication

I dedicate all my books to my wife Nicole, my four beautiful daughters, and the next generation.

*One generation shall praise Your works to another,
And shall declare Your mighty acts.*
— Psalm 145:4

Introduction

²²But the fruit of the Spirit is love, joy, peace, longsuffering, kindness, goodness, faithfulness, ²³gentleness, self-control. Against such there is no law.

– Galatians 5:22-23

Fruit is something that is cultivated. The Holy Spirit is doing a supernatural work in our lives to conform us to the character of Christ. The fruit of the Spirit is not just something we display, it's also something we experience from God. I experience the love of God, and I become more loving. I experience joy unspeakable, and I become full of joy. I enter into a peace that passes understanding, and I become more peaceful.

It's my prayer that as you go through this devotional, you go beyond head knowledge to experiential knowledge. It's not enough to just know that God is love; you must also experience the power of God's transforming love.

Most people want to be thought of as a warm, thoughtful, and loving person. Unless, of course, you're a hit man for the Mob, then you want to be feared because that would help you maintain job security. I know that I want to be a nice guy. Not just so people will like me, but I want to please God as well.

Years ago I worked as the Kitchen Manager for a restaurant, and one of my duties was to check in all deliveries. I had to make sure we had received everything we ordered, and that the truck driver or salesperson didn't try to pack the order with more than we ordered. One morning when a delivery truck pulled up, a new driver popped out of the truck. I introduced myself and inquired about the regular driver. He introduced himself and handed me a card. I was intrigued; a truck driver typically does not have his own card. As I took his card he said. "Hi, I'm Mike. I'm a nice guy." I then looked at his card and it said, "Mike, truly a nice guy." This was hilarious to me, and after a good belly laugh, we got along famously.

It would be nice if all we had to do was present a card about how loving we are, but we all know it isn't that easy. We have to cultivate the love of God in our lives and allow the Holy Spirit to do His supernatural work.

Some people seem to naturally be loving. They ooze with niceness. They probably watch Hallmark movies and puppy videos on YouTube. They easily weep when someone is in pain. They are the mercy-motivated among us. Then there are the majority of us who want to tell some folks, "Jesus loves you but the rest of us hate your guts." Warm sappy feelings of loving kindness are not our first sensation. We need help. We have issues.

There are extremes. There are imbalances. There is a ditch on both sides of the road. Some are so loving that they enable people in their sin. They think it is spiritual to lovingly affirm someone when what they need is a rebuke and some good ol' tough love. Then there are others who are too harsh when they should be more understanding. They think they are some kind of Old Testament prophet who believe they are to constantly remind folks what evil sinners unto the Lord they are. The book you have in your hand will help to bring some balance and understanding to the unfathomable depths of God's love. In the Holy Spirit's hands, it will cultivate more love fruit within our lives.

The Love of God

The love of God is so powerful that
it can heal any broken soul.
The love of God is not only the most
powerful force in the universe,
but it also passes knowledge.
It is so vast that it is
beyond comprehension.
~ Alan Leonhardt

Day 1

God's Love is the Foundation

*¹⁷That Christ may dwell in your hearts through faith; that you, **being rooted and grounded in love**, ¹⁸may be able to comprehend with all the saints what is the width and length and depth and height— ¹⁹**to know the love of Christ which passes knowledge; that you may be filled with all the fullness of God**.*
– Ephesians 3:17-19

The foundation of my relationship with God is love and trust. I know that He loves me and wants the best for me. My love has grown so deep that any sacrifice seems small in comparison to God's grace shone to me. My loyalty has been earned by God's demonstration, over and over, that He is wise and compassionate toward me. When I was in pain on the side of life's road, He found me and poured on the oil and the wine. When my sins had brought me low, and I was eating life's pig slop, He welcomed me home, forgave me, and restored me. I gave Him my brokenness and He made me a co-heir with Christ. He elevated me from the dunghill and set me among princes, even the princes of His people.

Love must be the foundation of your relationship with God. It can't just be that you are afraid of burning in eternal hell (although a little fear goes a long way…). The foundation of your relationship with God can't just be about what God can do for you. There is reward, and looking toward God's reward is part of faith. But if reward is all you're looking for, then what happens when you feel cheated? Or when you feel you deserve more than what God has given you? You may sell out to the highest bidder. Remember Judas Iscariot.

The Love of God

> *After these things the word of the Lord came to Abram in a vision, saying, "Do not be afraid, Abram. **I am your shield, your exceedingly great reward.**"*
> – *Genesis 15:1*

God, Himself, is my greatest reward. His lovingkindness is better than life.

As a young man, I got severely depressed over a failed romantic relationship. It was as though all the rejections of my entire life had piled onto that rejection, putting me into an emotional tailspin. The Holy Spirit was trying to renew my hope and gave me an amazing verse about hope and faith, but I still experienced down times.

One cold and rainy night, I was in a friend's truck heading home from an evening church meeting when one of my melancholy depressions descended on me. The despondency was so thick that it was sucking the oxygen out of the truck cab. My friend was a very spiritual man and he said, "Let's sing a song." I gave him a hideous look that conveyed these thoughts: "What are you, nuts? That's the last thing I want to do right now." He ignored my attempted intimidation and began singing.

Thy loving-kindness is better than life
Thy loving-kindness is better than life
My lips shall praise thee, thus I will bless thee
I will lift up my hands unto thy name.

I reluctantly joined in. After the second time through, something began to break over me. I felt the warm, liquid gold love of God being poured over my whole being. I began to weep and wail. God assured me that His love is greater than man's rejections. I'm not a person who cries often, as I had been taught that a man doesn't cry; he is tough and faces life with courage. However, I discovered that God can break me. His love can overwhelm me and cause me to weep like a child. There is something beautiful and heartwarming when I see a macho grown-man weep in the presence of God. I don't care how tough we are, every heart will melt when the love of God is poured out upon us.

Supernatural Love

One of life's basic needs is to be loved. Souls that never experience love are twisted and distorted into grotesque apparitions of humanity. Some of the evilest, ruthless, and brutal people in history were conditioned to hate. The love of God is so powerful that it can heal any broken soul. The love of God is not only the most powerful force in the universe, but it also passes knowledge. It is so vast that it is beyond comprehension. You and I are on a journey to know the love of God, to grow in the love of God, and to understand the intricacies and nuances of the love of God. The more we know by experience and understanding, the more we will be filled with God's fullness. Christians want more power and anointing to see people set free and to do the works of Christ. Ephesians 3:19 gives you the secret to a greater anointing:

> ...^{19}to know the love of Christ which passes knowledge; that you may be filled with all the fullness of God.

You must pray to know God's love MORE! Please pray with me:

Dear Heavenly Father,
Show me Your love. Help me to know Your love more and more.
Let me have Your love and compassion for others as well. I ask that You fill me with Your love now.
I love you, Lord. Where I lack understanding and balance, please correct me and instruct me.
I ask in Jesus' name, Amen

Day 2

God is Love

*⁷Beloved, let us love one another, for love is of God;
and everyone who loves is born of God and knows God.
⁸He who does not love does not know God, for **God is love**.*
— I John 4:7-8

Our God is called the God of hope *(see Romans 15:13)*, the God of all comfort *(see II Corinthians 1:3)*, and the God of peace *(see Romans 15:33)*, but I John 4:8 states that our God IS love. He is the embodiment of everything that love is. All of us have a perception and limited understanding of what love is, based on our life experiences. But God is the eternal definition of ALL that love is. We will forever be experiencing and growing in our understanding of God's love.

When you came to know God, what you experienced was love in its purest form. God loves you even when you are unlovable. God's love is deeply honest. He knows everything about you and still has an honest and pure love for you. His love isn't an infatuation based on what He imagines or hopes you are like; He honestly loves you because He *is* love. And then He expects us to have the same love that we experience from Him, and to show that to others! Wow!

The greatest demonstration of God's love was the passion of Christ. Whenever you are tempted to doubt God's love and concern for you, consider the love God expressed in sending His only begotten Son to die for *your* sins. He loved you and died for you before you even knew about His love. He died for you even when there was no guarantee that you would return His love. This is the greatest example of true love.

> *⁹In this the love of God was manifested toward us,
> that God has sent His only begotten Son into the world,
> that we might live through Him. ¹⁰In this is love,
> not that we loved God, but that He loved us and sent His
> Son to be the propitiation for our sins. ¹¹Beloved, if God so
> loved us, we also ought to love one another.*
> *– I John 4:9-11*

Years ago, I made a friend during one of my first Bible college classes. She was a very fun person and a new Christian with a lot of fresh fire for the Lord. She wanted to tell her ex-live-in boyfriend about how her life had changed since she became a born-again Christian. Unfortunately, she ended up being seduced and falling into sin, and she spiraled down into a depression. She felt so condemned and like such a failure as a new Christian. She called me and wanted to meet at a restaurant to confess her sin and have me pray with her. The last thing she needed was someone to rub her face in her failure. She already knew she had sinned and wanted restoration. The Lord gave me this Bible verse to encourage her:

> *¹⁷How precious also are Your thoughts to me, O God!
> How great is the sum of them!
> ¹⁸If I should count them, they would be more in number than the sand;
> When I awake, I am still with You.*
> *– Psalm 139:17-18*

I told her, "God thinks a lot about you. He thinks more thoughts about you than there are grains of sand on the seashore. You have to love someone an awful lot to think that much about them. You are so loved by God that He is not going to give up on you because you stumbled. We are all a work in progress. I'm NOT saying that your sin does not matter. You've already been spanked by your own conscience. Thank God you feel some remorse, some people do not. Let's pray and receive God's forgiveness and restoration."

She began to weep and thank me for reminding her of God's great love. We prayed together and she was refreshed. Then I advised her not to visit her ex-boyfriend again, and that we would pray for him.

The Love of God

I encouraged her to never put herself in a compromising situation, to stay away from temptation, and that God can send someone else to witness to him.

To know the God of the Bible is to know more of what true love is. Please pray with me to know God's love.

Dear Heavenly Father,
Show me Your love in deeper ways than I have experienced. My understanding is so limited. I want to know You more. I want to experience Your love and compassion. I want to have a greater compassion for others as a result. Expand my heart and capacity to comprehend Your great love.
In Jesus' name, Amen

Day 3

There is No Fear in Love

There is no fear in love; but perfect love casts out fear, because fear involves torment. But he who fears has not been made perfect in love.
— I John 4:18

Years ago, there was a man who started coming to our church, and I didn't like him. He was a very brilliant engineer, but the problem was that he knew it all too well. He frequently came across as very arrogant and condescending. He was also good looking and in perfect physical shape, and it just bugged me. They say you hate in others what you see in yourself, so I guess I can come across as a little bit arrogant at times myself. It's hard to be humble when you think you're the smartest guy in the room.

One night, during that time when I was struggling with my relationship with that man, I had a dream. I was looking at a computer screen and the screensaver was scrolling a phrase back and forth across the screen: "There is no fear in love, there is no fear in love." And then that man's face appeared on the screen. I woke up and just knew what God was trying to say to me. The Holy Spirit was revealing to me that my insecurities regarding that man were fear-based. The reason I didn't like him was because of MY insecurities, and if I would just love him it would be okay. The Holy Spirit was right.

There is a grace to love people. Love overcomes our fears and insecurities. If we will love them with the supernatural love of God, then we are safe to be vulnerable and authentic. There is no inferiority in the love of God. These principles will work in our marriages and all relationships where we desire to go deeper.

The Love of God

There is no fear in love. There is something stronger than faith and hope in conquering our fears. Love. We have a weak image of God's love, and yet it is the most powerful force in the universe.

Love never fails. Love is not insecure. Love drives us to go beyond human limitations and perform herculean feats. Love endures ALL.

The foundation of our relationship with God must be love. He first loved us and our response to such a magnificent and perfect love toward us is to ultimately love back. He loves us in our rebellion. He loves us when we don't love ourselves. He loves us when we are being mean and nasty. How can this be? Can God hate sin and love deeply the sinner? The reason he hates the sin is that *it hurts the sinner.*

Please pray with me.

Dear Heavenly Father,
I ask Your forgiveness for letting my insecurities damage
friendships. I want to be secure in Your love. Help me to be fearless
in Your love. Fill me with Your love today so that I will be free of
inferiorities. I want to be confident in Your love for me. If there
are any lies about the nature of your love that I am believing,
please reveal them and set me free.
I ask in the precious name of Jesus, Amen

Day 4

The Compassion of God

*The Lord is gracious and full of **compassion**,
Slow to anger and great in mercy.*
— Psalm 145:8

*Through the Lord's mercies we are not consumed,
Because His compassions fail not.*
— Lamentations 3:22

And when Jesus went out He saw a great multitude; and He was moved with compassion for them, and healed their sick.
— Matthew 14:14

Some of the greatest miracles of Jesus' ministry were motivated by His compassion.

- Blind men were healed *(see Matthew 20:34)*
- Food was multiplied for a multitude *(see Mark 8:2)*
- A widow's dead son was brought back to life *(see Luke 7:13)*

We can have faith in God's compassion. Sometimes God will do a miracle because of His love and compassion. It has nothing to do with our great faith or righteousness. I started to see this connection between God's supernatural compassion and the release of His miracle power when I went on a short-term mission trip to Lima, Peru.

The year was 2000, and when we arrived in Lima my team and I prayed for God's heart of love and compassion for the people of Peru. I know God answered that prayer because I actually felt something; you don't realize how hard your heart is until you actually feel the

The Love of God

heart of God. I went on that mission trip out of duty, faithfulness, and discipline. There is nothing wrong with doing things by faith, and not always because you feel something, but it's nice when you do feel something.

We were driving down the busy city streets, and as I observed the people going about their business, I began to weep and have a sincere burden for them. This took me by surprise because I didn't know I could feel the compassion of God like that.

One time I was sharing the gospel message at a park. A crowd had gathered and I had an interpreter with me. As I was wrapping up my short message, I could feel the compassion of God for the people drop onto the meeting. A man in the crowd started to shout, so I asked the interpreter what he was saying. He is saying "I am healed! I am healed! I have no pain!" I hadn't even gotten to the healing part of my message yet, or finished my invitation to believe in Christ. I asked the healed man to come forward so that I could speak with him. It turned out that he had been in an advanced stage of Lou Gehrig's disease, used a cane, and was barely able to walk to the meeting in the park. The compassion of God came upon that man, and He healed him instantly. This was a true creative miracle. Not only did the pain leave, but strength returned to that man's dilapidated muscles. Praise God!

This was a huge lesson for me. The compassion of God is an important key to the release of His miracle-working power. You and I need to flow in the love of God if we want to see people set free. We need God's heart for people, with a true and sincere love for the people we are called to serve. Otherwise our love can grow cold, and then we can go through the motions with no passion.

Let's pray for God's compassion today:

Dear God,
Please fill my heart with Your love for others. Let me feel Your compassion for the people around me. Renew my compassion for my family, work mates, community, and church.

*Fill me today. I don't want to go on without a heart of love. Let my heart burn afresh with Your love and passion for a lost, hurting, and dying world.
In Jesus' precious name, Amen*

Day 5

God is Good

¹³Indeed it came to pass, when the trumpeters and singers were as one, to make one sound to be heard in praising and thanking the Lord, and when they lifted up their voice with the trumpets and cymbals and instruments of music, and praised the Lord, saying: ***"For He is good, For His mercy endures forever,"*** *that the house, the house of the Lord, was filled with a cloud, ¹⁴so that the priests could not continue ministering because of the cloud; for the glory of the Lord filled the house of God.*
– II Chronicles 5:13-14

One of the great lies that Satan and false religion likes to spread is that God is not loving and good. God gets blamed for a lot of things that He does not do. The great healing evangelist, Oral Roberts, defied the religious thinking in his day by coining a simple phrase, *"God is a good God and the devil is a bad devil."* It was popular in the 1950s to blame God for every sickness, war, and trouble. "If God is responsible for war atrocities, then how can He be good?" Has anyone ever asked you that? "If God is so good, why are there wars?" God actually answered that question in the Bible:

¹Where do wars and fights come from among you? Do they not come from your desires for pleasure that war in your members? ²You lust and do not have. You murder and covet and cannot obtain. You fight and war. Yet you do not have because you do not ask.
– James 4:1-2

Wars and their atrocities are because of man's sinful and evil nature. WE cause wars. One nation is greedy and wants something that belongs to another nation or a people group, so they start a war.

There will be a great day when God will cause all wars to cease:

> He shall judge between the nations, and rebuke many people;
> they shall beat their swords into plowshares, and their spears
> into pruning hooks; nation shall not lift up sword against nation,
> **neither shall they learn war anymore.**
> – Isaiah 2:4

> **He makes wars cease to the end of the earth;** He breaks the bow
> and cuts the spear in two; He burns the chariot in the fire.
> – Psalm 46:9

Death, sickness, war, and all the terrible tragedies of this life came into the world because of man's sinfulness against God. Never forget that God is the fountainhead of good. Even when He judges, it's for our good. The devil, the world system, and our sinful nature are the perpetrators of death and destruction.

> **Every good gift and every perfect gift** *is from above,
> and comes down from the Father of lights,
> with whom there is no variation or shadow of turning.*
> – James 1:17

We must acknowledge that God's loving goodness and His glory will fill the temple. It's when they sang, *"For He is good! For His mercy endures forever!"* that God responded with a thick cloud of glory *(see II Chronicles 5:13)*. When I read about the glory cloud that filled the Azusa Street warehouse, circa 1907, and the miracles that resulted, I get so hungry for this manifestation of God's supernatural love.

I want you to do an exercise to break off a chain of lies. The devil has lied to you. Satan has stolen from you, and hurt you, and then blamed God. This has injured your relationship with your heavenly Father. You have borne the burden of this blame for a long time. Declare this with me several times, and chains will be broken. You will be filled with God's glory in your inner temple; your spirit. Even if you don't think this applies to you, do it anyway.

The Love of God

Worship the Lord with this and declare it several times. Sing it if you want.

For He is good! And His mercy endures forever!
For He is good! And His mercy endures forever!
For He is good! And His mercy endures forever!

Day 6

The Passion

But God demonstrates His own love toward us, in that while we were still sinners, Christ died for us.
– Romans 5:8

¹⁶For God so loved the world that He gave His only begotten Son, that whoever believes in Him should not perish but have everlasting life. ¹⁷For God did not send His Son into the world to condemn the world, but that the world through Him might be saved.
– John 3:16-17

Have you ever had someone ask you, "If God is so loving, how could He send people to hell?" Actually, God loves people so much that He died a horrible death on a Roman cross to keep people *from* hell. Whenever God's love is on trial, remember 'The Passion'.

The Catholic Church first called the volunteer, vicarious death that Jesus suffered, The Passion. From the Latin verb *patior, passus sum*, "to suffer, bear, endure." This is from which we get our words patience and patient. Depending on one's views, the Passion may also include the events leading up to the cross; His betrayer, trial, and beatings.

Mel Gibson's 2004 movie, "The Passion of the Christ", starring Jim Caviezel, was the highest-grossing Christian film of all time, grossing $612 million worldwide, and it cost $30 million to make. The film is R-rated for the personal violence it portrayed. The whipping, beatings, and crucifixion scenes were so brutal and bloody that the personal violence almost upstaged the message of the film. No other film of Christ's death comes close to the reality of the kind of death that Christ suffered. Someone commented to me that they didn't believe

The Love of God

Christ's death was as bad as that film portrayed. My response was that the death of Christ was even worse than "The Passion of the Christ" portrayed. I know this because of what the prophet Isaiah said:

> [13] *Behold, My Servant shall deal prudently; He shall be exalted and extolled and be very high.* [14] ***Just as many were astonished at you, So His visage was marred more than any man, And His form more than the sons of men;*** [15] *So shall He sprinkle many nations. Kings shall shut their mouths at Him; For what had not been told them they shall see, and what they had not heard they shall consider.*
> — Isaiah 52:13-15

According to Isaiah 52:14, Jesus was tortured and beaten to the point that He was unrecognizable as a human being, thus depicting the length, depth, and width of the love of God. The unfathomable measure of the love of Jesus to go through such suffering so that you and I could have access to God, and so that you and I could be forgiven of all sin and have eternal life. Never doubt the love of God and the length to which God will go for you. Whenever you begin to doubt whether you are loved, think of the Passion.

> *How much more shall the blood of Christ, who through the eternal Spirit offered Himself without spot to God, cleanse your conscience from dead works to serve the living God?*
> — Hebrews 9:14

In the Old Testament, the sacrificed blood of bulls and goats would cover man's sin. With the New Testament, the sacrificed blood of Christ does more than just cover your sin, it takes sin away, breaks the power of sin over your life, and cleanses you from your sin. Hallelujah! Praise the Lord! You can be delivered, forgiven, and born again.

> *If we confess our sins, He is faithful and just to forgive us our sins and to cleanse us from all unrighteousness.*
> — I John 1:9

How do we respond to such love? Another question is, how can you *not* respond to such love? This love is beyond this world. It takes a God-encounter to even begin to grasp it. Let's pray together that people will see and experience this love. No one can choose Hell when they understand even a portion of God's rich love.

Dear Father God,
Help me never to doubt Your love for me. Continue to show me and remind me of Your great love for me. Help others around me to experience Your love. Thank you, Jesus, for the Passion. I have an eternal record of Your great love in all four Gospels. I have a record in my heart because I have personally experienced Your love. I will continue to pray for the lost around me. Help me to have the right words to give witness to Your saving grace.
In Jesus' name, Amen.

Day 7

The Parable of the Good Samaritan

Please read the entire account of the Parable of the Good Samaritan found in Luke 10:25-37

³³But a certain Samaritan, as he journeyed, came where he was. And when he saw him, he had compassion. ³⁴So he went to him and bandaged his wounds, pouring on oil and wine; and he set him on his own animal, brought him to an inn, and took care of him.
— Luke 10:33-34

Although this parable is meant to illustrate the way we should love our neighbor, it also demonstrates, in Technicolor, the love of God in action. The love of God is not a simple concept to be explained in a sterile *intellectual* fashion; it is to be demonstrated as well. The supernatural love of God is experienced.

As a teenager, I decided I was going to read the entire New Testament. Although I had been to Sunday School and was required to memorize Bible verses, I had never actually read through the Bible. As I was reading the Beatitudes in the 5th chapter of Matthew's Gospel, I was struck by the raw goodness of the ideals; I experienced a revelation from heaven. I realized that this book did not originate with men, it was just too good. It had to have come from a loving God. By nature, we are too evil to have invented things like the beatitudes, or the Parable of the Good Samaritan.

The main point of the Parable of the Good Samaritan is to teach us to be kind and loving to people who are helpless. What if we looked at the parable from a different perspective? If we are the helpless victim wounded by the side of the road, and Jesus is the Good Samaritan, a lesson emerges about the amazing love of God.

You and I are like the wounded victim by the side of the road, languishing in abandonment and the painful wounds of hard times. Most people don't come to the Lord when they are on top of the world, they must reach their bottom first. It's hard to appreciate the love of God unless you find yourself needing an abundant supply of mercy. God doesn't have to bring about our demise, or cause bad so He can show us His goodness. He just patiently waits for an opportunity to rescue us from our own folly.

There are four reasons that cause all nasty bad things to happen to mankind:

1. **Personal sin:** The wages of sin are death *(see Romans 6:23)*. Sin carries its own death and destruction. Eventually, your sin will find you out, and you will have to collect your wages.

2. **Sin in the world:** Mankind is sinful *(see Isaiah 53:6, Romans 3:23)*. The world system is mostly anti-Christ. People are mean. We often suffer from the sins of others. Death, sickness and injustice are in the world because of sin.

3. **Satan and demons:** There are evil spiritual presences in the world, and their modus operandi is to steal, kill and destroy *(see John 10:10)*. Without the protection and covering of God, you are at their mercy.

4. **The righteous judgment of God:** When God brings an act of judgment, it is righteous and holy. A few incidents of God's righteous judgment come to mind: Sodom and Gomorrah *(see Genesis 18-19)*, Noah's flood *(see Genesis 6-9)*, and Ananias and Sapphira *(see Acts 5:1-11)*. A child of God does not have to fear this kind of judgment. It is reserved for the most rebellious and hardened sinners.

We are like the beat-up victim on the side of life's road. The vicious and ruthless rage of sin and hard times has found us. The selfish hardhearted souls of mankind will not help us in our defeat and shame. Jesus is like the Good Samaritan. He finds us in our wounded state and

The Love of God

binds up our wounds. He pours on the oil and the wine. He puts us on His mule and takes us to the local inn (the local church). He gives the innkeeper money to nurse the wayfaring traveler back to health, and then He tells the Pastor, "Take care of him, and whatever more you spend, when I come again (the Second Coming), I will repay you." That is how great God's love is toward me and you.

> *He stooped down to lift me out of danger from the desolate pit I was in, out of the muddy mess I had fallen into. Now he's lifted me up into a firm, secure place and steadied me while I walk along his ascending path.*
> *– Psalm 40:2 TPT*

Just begin to thank Him for His love. Use your own words; you can begin with: *For You are good, and Your mercy endures forever.*

Accessing God's Love

Our God is love.
He is the fountainhead of all the unselfish
nobility and courage that true love is.
~ Alan Leonhardt

Day 8

Courageous Love

¹³Watch, stand fast in the faith, be brave, be strong.
¹⁴Let all that you do be done with love.
— I Corinthians 16:13-14

Love takes courage. When a mother gets up before her children, gets them ready for school, and makes them lunches before she starts her day; that's courageous love. When a man pushes himself at work so that he can earn a promotion to bring something extra home to provide for his family; that is courageous love.

In 1945, during World War II, a battle raged for Japan's island of Okinawa, and the key to winning this battle was the Maeda escarpment, nicknamed "Hacksaw Ridge". The battlefield was located on top of a sheer 400-foot cliff where the Japanese were well fortified with a network of machine gun nests and booby traps. There was a young American medic named Desmond Ross, a devout Christian and a conscientious objector who refused to carry a weapon or kill anyone. The battalion to which Desmond was assigned was beaten back by the Japanese and ordered to retreat to the bottom of the cliff. Desmond refused to leave any men behind, so he repeatedly ran back into the kill zone and carried wounded to the cliff's edge, and then lowered them down one at a time. Each time he saved a man's life he would pray out loud, "Lord, please help me get one more." By the end of that night, it is estimated that Desmond Ross saved 75 men. He was the first conscientious objector to be awarded the Medal of Honor for bravery on the battlefield. A movie was made in 2016 depicting this true event, starring Andrew Garfield and directed by Mel Gibson. The film was aptly named "Hacksaw Ridge".

Supernatural Love

Most of us will never have our love and courage put to the test in such a dramatic arena like a pacific island battle during World War II. But, at some point, all of us will have to reach deep down inside and pull out the love and courage needed to face one of life's great challenges. What about the love it takes to become a caregiver for someone who has had a terrible accident, suffers from a debilitating disease, or is at death's door? What about college students burning the midnight oil for a respectable grade to make their parents proud? If truth be told, the hidden power of supernatural love is the prime mover for much of the selfless beauty of our world. It cannot be seen with the naked eye, and yet it has motivated nations and armies. The *greatest* selfless act of love was this:

> [16]**For God so loved the world** that He gave His only begotten Son, that whoever believes in Him should not perish but have everlasting life. [17]For God did not send His Son into the world to condemn the world, but that the world through Him might be saved.
> – John 3:16-17

> [7]For scarcely for a righteous man will one die; yet perhaps for a good man someone would even dare to die. [8]But **God demonstrates His own love toward us**, in that while we were still sinners, Christ died for us.
> – Romans 5:7-8

> Greater love has no one than this, than to lay down one's life for his friends.
> – John 15:13

Our God is love. He is the fountainhead of all the unselfish nobility and courage that true love is. As we draw closer to the Source, we can hope to receive an impartation that will help us to become better human beings. For all the ugliness, violence, and pure evil that exists in this world, there is love's pure light which will never dim. It will remain a beacon of hope and strength until the end of the age. The deeper the darkness, the brighter the candle's light. The darkness will never extinguish the courageous radiance of God's amazing love.

Accessing God's Love

[1]Arise, shine; For your light has come! And the glory of the Lord is risen upon you. [2]For behold, the darkness shall cover the earth, and deep darkness the people; but the Lord will arise over you, and His glory will be seen upon you.
— Isaiah 60:1-2

Day 9

Love is Not Easily Offended

*⁴Love suffers long and is kind; love does not envy;
love does not parade itself, is not puffed up;
⁵does not behave rudely, does not seek its own,*
is not provoked, *thinks no evil; ⁶does not rejoice in
iniquity, but rejoices in the truth; ⁷bears all things, believes
all things, hopes all things, endures all things.*
— I Corinthians 13:4-7

One day I was reading the characteristics of love in this "love" chapter, and the phrase *"is not provoked"* jumped out at me. When I think of love, kindness, and longsuffering, I never think of not being easily offended. And yet, if a person is living out the supernatural love of God, they are hard to offend.

Some folks are what I call "drama junkies." They are always looking for a fight. They are so accustomed to constant drama and upheaval happening all around them that if things are too peaceful, they have to stir something up. Are you a person that's always at war with someone? Does the slightest perceived insult set you off? *"What did you mean by that?" "Why did he look at me like that?" "I deserve respect."*

It's interesting that Jesus predicted that in the last days the love of many will wax cold, and because of this, offense would increase.

¹⁰And then **many will be offended**, *will betray one another, and will* **hate one another**. *¹¹Then many false prophets will rise up and deceive many. ¹²****And because lawlessness will abound, the love of many will grow cold***. *¹³But he who endures to the end shall be saved.*
— Matthew 24:10-13

Accessing God's Love

It's very interesting how being offended is connected with a cold, unloving heart. People that are abounding in God's love are secure. They know that they are loved by God very deeply, so petty insults don't affect them. That's not to say we should ignore rude behavior. But when you are secure in God's love, offenses don't seem to affect you so personally. Rudeness can be dealt with in a much calmer and rational way. A way that will lead to de-escalation and not to a backwood, blood-feud.

Years ago, I was leading a home-prayer meeting. The host loved the King James translation of the Bible. In fact, he had much of the Bible memorized in King James English. As we prayed for one another, he would often give a Bible verse to the person being prayed for. The Bible verses were very prophetic and were spot on with what the person needed. One evening I was being prayed for because I was dealing with an offense. I hadn't shared with anyone at the meeting that I was upset about a betrayal. When you are the Pastor, you can't talk negatively about people, nor can you always share certain struggles with church members. The host of the prayer meeting pulled a King James Bible verse out and quoted it to me: *Great peace have they which love thy law: And nothing shall offend them. Psalm 119:165*

I was simply amazed at how accurate this verse was to my situation. God was comforting me. He was telling me to be at peace, and that I was too dignified to sulk for too long. I am a lover of the Word of God, and that Word gives me strength. I just needed to forgive, bless, and move on. God would deal with the betrayer. Because of this Bible verse, I was able to accept God's grace to overcome and not overreact.

Are you struggling with offenses? Let's pray for God's wisdom in how to deal with them. Let's ask for an outpouring of God's love so that offenses do not bring us down.

Dear God,
You said that if we needed wisdom that we could ask You, and You would give it liberally. I am asking now for Your great wisdom. You see the offenses that are hurting me and causing anger and

stress. Please show me the best response. I know I have to forgive, but do I need to confront this or just move on? Should I just let this go, or should I try to work this out? Show me the way of true love and peace.
In Jesus' name I pray, Amen

> [17] *But the wisdom that is from above is first pure, then peaceable, gentle, willing to yield, full of mercy and good fruits, without partiality and without hypocrisy.* [18] *Now the fruit of righteousness is sown in peace by those who make peace.*
> *– James 3:17-18*

Day 10

Love Fulfills the Law

*For all **the law is fulfilled** in one word, even in this:*
"You shall love your neighbor as yourself."
— *Galatians 5:14*

Owe no one anything except to love one another,
*for he who loves another **has fulfilled the law**.*
— *Romans 13:8*

The Old Testament contains a total of 613 commandments. The commandments, or mitzvahs, cover many aspects of daily life, including family, personal hygiene, and diet. Could it really be that easy to just walk in the love of Christ and fulfill all the law?

Well, let's think about that – If I love someone and want the best for them, then I will be willing to sacrifice for their wellbeing. Why do Fathers work hard and give up personal wants so that their family can be provided for? Love. Why do mothers rise early to make sure their children have a lunch for school? Love. Why did God send His only Son to teach us His ways and to be a sacrifice for our sins? *Amazing love.*

If we truly love someone, we will not take advantage of them sexually. In the era in which we are living, people are so confused about how love is expressed.

> ³*For this is the will of God, your sanctification: that you should abstain from sexual immorality;* ⁴*that each of you should know how to possess his own vessel in sanctification and honor,* ⁵*not in passion of lust, like the Gentiles who do not know God;* ⁶*that no one should take advantage of and defraud his brother in this matter, because the Lord is the*

> *avenger of all such, as we also forewarned you and testified.*
> *⁷For God did not call us to uncleanness, but in holiness.*
> *⁸Therefore he who rejects this does not reject man, but God, who has also given us His Holy Spirit.*
> *I Thessalonians 4:3-8*

I was the chaplain for a Christian school in the late 1990s. I taught a Bible class that the High School students could take for course credit. I was teaching on sexual purity and how to manage yourself sexually. My course material was based on I Thessalonians 4:3-8. As I expounded and defined sexual immorality, and all the practices that fall into that category, many were surprised to discover that premarital sex was a sin. I kid you not. These "Christian" young people had never been taught that fornication was wrong. They knew that adultery was wrong, and they even knew that the Bible was against homosexuality, but in their minds, sex before marriage was okay. Think about it. Everything in our culture promotes sex, sex, and more sex outside of marriage. Our culture pushes cohabitation before marriage. It is now the norm that the accepted step just before marriage is to live together.

After reasoning with my students about all the reasons premarital sex is wrong and harmful (STDs, babies out of wedlock, soul ties, and having a hard heart that carries into marriage, etc.), I came to the bottom line; the main reason it's wrong is that it will cause harm to yourself and someone else. If I truly love someone, I will not cause them harm. I definitely will not try and selfishly take advantage of them. If I care about someone's relationship with God, I will not lead them into sin and harm their conscience. Love fulfills the law and does no harm to your neighbor.

> *¹⁰He who loves his brother abides in the light, and there is no cause for stumbling in him. ¹¹But he who hates his brother is in darkness and walks in darkness, and does not know where he is going, because the darkness has blinded his eyes.*
> *– I John 2:10-11*

Love not only fulfills the law, but when you are walking in God's supernatural love, there is no cause for stumbling in you. Why would

Accessing God's Love

there be so many encouragements to love one another in the New testament if we just naturally loved? You and I must reach out for God's grace to be loving. These exhortations are not to love the world, they are to Christians to love other Christians! We all know we should love sinners and desire to see people experience the love of God. You and I need many reminders to love our brothers and sisters in Christ.

Since you have purified your souls in obeying the truth through the Spirit in sincere love of the brethren, love one another fervently with a pure heart.
— I Peter 1:22

Finally, all of you be of one mind, having compassion for one another; love as brothers, be tenderhearted, be courteous.
— I Peter 3:8

8And above all things have fervent love for one another, for "love will cover a multitude of sins."
9Be hospitable to one another without grumbling.
— I Peter 4:8-9

Beloved, if God so loved us, we also ought to love one another.
— I John 4:11

Please pray with me:

Dear God, help my motives to be love. Thank You for the simplicity of serving You by just walking in true love toward others. Forgive me for complicating things. There is no cause for stumbling in me if my motive is love. Fill me this day with a love that is beyond me. Fill me with your supernatural love.
Thank you.
In Jesus' name I pray, Amen.

Day 11

The Spirit of Love

*For God has not given us a spirit of fear,
but of power and **of love** and of a sound mind.*
— II Timothy 1:7

*For God will never give you the spirit of fear, but **the Holy Spirit who gives you mighty power, love,** and self-control.*
— II Timothy 1:7 The Passion Translation

It's the Holy Spirit who infuses us with supernatural love, power to overcome, and soundness in our mind and emotions. If you could live in perfect love, you wouldn't need the Holy Spirit, but the truth is, we all fall short many times.

*Now hope does not disappoint, because **the love of God has been poured out in our hearts by the Holy Spirit who was given to us**.*
— Romans 5:5

We are all capable of natural love; love for family, friendship, romantic love, etc.. But even in these relationships, we can fall short. We need to reach for the grace in order to love beyond natural affection, to love people with the love of the Lord, and to love our spouse and children in a self-sacrificing way that goes beyond any feelings or commitments.

If you fail to reach for the love of the Holy Spirit, there is a danger of other things slipping in to erode your love. Unforgiveness, bitterness, malice, and envy are sins of the heart that war against your love walk. You will always have opportunities to hate and hold grudges. Some people are so vindictive that they hold grudges for years. I met a woman at a healing conference who was healed and set free of arthritis and many other serious things *after* she released forgiveness. I asked her who she had to forgive, and she confessed to having a notebook that contained over a hundred people that she had serious ought against. WOW! This woman held on to slights all the way back to grade school. She remembered every name and wrote them down so she could forgive each and every one of them.

> *Looking carefully lest anyone fall short of the grace of God;*
> *lest any root of bitterness springing up cause trouble,*
> *and by this many become defiled.*
> *– Hebrews 12:15*

Have you ever met a truly bitter Christian? It's so sad. What is even sadder is when they justify their spiteful attitude with the Bible. *There is nothing so distasteful as a Christian justifying hate by twisting the scriptures.* I have met senior saints that have not matured well. Instead of having an attractive beautiful spirit in old age, they are mean in a religious way and bitter. Don't you want to finish your race well?

In the western novel, Lonesome Dove by Larry McMurtry, there is an old Texas Ranger named Augustus McCrae. He often says in the novel, "The older the violin, the sweeter the music." That's the way it should be with all Christians. Our spirit should grow sweeter with age and experience.

A dear friend of my family just passed on to glory. We called her Grandma Judy. She was a surrogate grandma to my children. She was so sweet that it almost made you doubt your salvation. She allowed nothing to make her bitter. She weeded the garden of her heart often and, by God's grace, was able to emanate the love of Jesus until her death. God bless you Grandma Judy.

> [30]*And do not grieve the Holy Spirit of God, by whom you were sealed for the day of redemption.* [31]*Let all bitterness, wrath, anger, clamor, and evil speaking be put away from you, with all malice.* [32]*And be kind to one another, tenderhearted, forgiving one another, even as God in Christ forgave you.*
> *– Ephesians 4:30-32*

Supernatural Love

Do you see how we can grieve the Holy Spirit by holding on to bitterness and unforgiveness? Clamor is loud arguing, and malice is harboring ill will toward others.

So how do we forgive? We forgive by faith. Tell the Lord that you choose to forgive "so and so." When you think of someone and you get angry, forgive them by faith. When you think of them again and you get angry, continue to forgive by faith. Eventually, your feelings will line up with your confession.

The Holy Spirit empowers us to love others. He teaches us how to love. We are insufficient on our own to love purely. God is able to bring increase to our love walk and teach us to love better.

> *And may the Lord make you increase and abound in love to one another and to all, just as we do to you.*
> *— I Thessalonians 3:12*

> *But concerning brotherly love you have no need that I should write to you, for you yourselves are taught by God to love one another.*
> *— I Thessalonians 4:9*

Please pray with me to forgive and abound in the supernatural love of God:

Dear Father in Heaven, I forgive by faith all who have offended me. Forgive me for holding anger and grudges toward them. Fill me with your love by the power of the Holy Spirit. Thank You, Holy Spirit, for teaching me to abound in love. I open my heart to hear Your voice and be taught to love more effectively. In the name of Jesus, Amen.

Day 12

Leaving Your First Love

Nevertheless I have this against you, that you have left your first love.
— Revelation 2:4

(Please read the whole letter to the church of Ephesus, Revelation 2:1-7)

Chapters 2 and 3 of the Revelation of Jesus Christ are letters that Jesus commanded the holy Apostle John to write to seven churches in Asia. What is amazing about these seven churches is that every church today fits into one of those churches. The seven churches encapsulate the church-age. You can find the church that you attend in one of these churches.

Another amazing thing about the seven churches is that every Christian is like one of those churches. If you have been through persecution, then you can identify with the church of Smyrna. If you are a lukewarm and apathetic Christian, then you are the church of Laodicea. If you have lost your passion and fervent love for God, then you are the Ephesian church.

Only two of the seven churches received no correction or reproof from our Savior; Smyrna, the persecuted church, and Philadelphia, the church of brotherly love. The church that I most want to identify with is the church of Philadelphia. They are the faithful and persevering saints that keep their hearts with all diligence. Malice and bitterness have no place to take root in their hearts, and they will be delivered from the hour of trial that will overtake the entire earth. Because you are reading a devotional about supernatural love, I believe that you want to maintain your heart of love also, and want to remain in the church of Philadelphia; the church of brotherly love.

Supernatural Love

I want to draw out a lesson from the letter to the church of Ephesus. Why did Jesus tell them that they had left their first love? Have *you* become stale and distant in your relationship with your Savior?

When we look at the church of Ephesus, we see that Jesus begins by affirming them. I like the way Jesus tells us what we are doing right before He corrects us.

> ²*I know your works, your labor, your patience, and that you cannot bear those who are evil. And you have tested those who say they are apostles and are not, and have found them liars; ³and you have persevered and have patience, and have labored for My name's sake and have not become weary.*
> *– Revelation 2:2-3*

After reading these affirmations, you start to wonder what could possibly be wrong here? They did good works, they persevered, they knew the Word good enough to test false apostles, and they lived for Christ. And yet Jesus tells them that they had left their first love. Somehow these sincere believers grew stale and parched. They went through all the robotic motions of being a Christian, but their passion had dulled. Some of their relatives are alive in a church near you. In fact, it could be you. Have you known Christians who go to church out of habit and duty, but they don't feel anything anymore? They have become cynical and skeptical, saying things like:

- "I've heard it all."
- "Oh, it's just another evangelist."
- "Why do we have to worship for so long, let's just sing a couple of choruses and get to the teaching."
- "Here comes another missionary begging for money."
- "I've done my time, don't ask me to volunteer."

What happened to them (and you)? You were so on fire for God at one time. You used to hunger for the Word of God. You used to weep during the worship service as you poured out your heart to God.

Accessing God's Love

It reminds me of that old song by the Righteous Brothers, "You've lost that lovin' feelin'." How do you get the fire back?

> [4] *Nevertheless I have this against you, that you have left your first love.* [5] ***Remember therefore from where you have fallen; repent and do the first works,*** *or else I will come to you quickly and remove your lampstand from its place—unless you repent.*
> – Revelation 2:4-5

Do you want the passion back? God has not moved, you have. God has not stopped loving you with a consuming passion. He's crazy about you. It's you who have allowed the world to creep in. "Do not love the world or the things in the world. If anyone loves the world, the love of the Father is not in him" (I John 2:15). What *is* loving the world? It is anything that dulls your relationship and passion for God and His kingdom.

To repent means to change your mind and turn from what you know is wrong. God is calling you back to a real, exciting, and adventurous love relationship with Him. Don't settle for just having eternal life insurance and going through the motions. Knowing God personally IS eternal life.

> *And this is eternal life, that they may know You, the only true God, and Jesus Christ whom You have sent.*
> – John 17:3

> *Therefore say to them, 'Thus says the Lord of hosts: "Return to Me," says the Lord of hosts, "and I will return to you," says the Lord of hosts.*
> – Zechariah 1:3

> *Job answered God: "I'm convinced: You can do anything and everything. Nothing and no one can upset your plans. You asked, 'Who is this muddying the water, ignorantly confusing the issue, second-guessing my purposes?' I admit it. I was the one. I babbled on about things far beyond me, made small talk about wonders way over my head. You told me, 'Listen, and let me do the talking. Let me ask the questions. You give the answers.'* ***I admit I once lived by rumors of you; now I have it all firsthand—from my own eyes and ears!***

*I'm sorry—forgive me. I'll never do that again, I promise!
I'll never again live on crusts of hearsay, crumbs of rumor."*
– Job 42:1-6 *The Message*

Prayer:

Oh God, please forgive me for allowing my passion to slip. I love You. Search my heart. Whatever You want me to give up I will. I put You first. You are my first love. Fill me with Your love now. In the name of Your holy Son, Jesus, Amen.

Day 13

Pray in the Holy Spirit

²⁰But you, beloved, building yourselves up on your most holy faith,
praying in the Holy Spirit, *²¹**keep yourselves in the love of God**,*
looking for the mercy of our Lord Jesus Christ unto eternal life.
— *Jude 1:20-21*

Praying in tongues will not only build your faith, it will also keep you in the love of God!

When we pray in the Holy Spirit, we are praying in total sync with God's will. Have you ever felt such a connection with the Holy Spirit in prayer that your prayer was like a prophecy? You were praying prophetic prayers. This can be done in your known language or while praying in a heavenly language.

I sometimes challenge people to pray in tongues for just 20 minutes. If you can pray in the Spirit for at least 20 minutes you will feel the recharge of your faith. It's the promise of Jude 20. I pray in tongues on and off throughout my day, every day; when doing chores, when driving my car, whenever I feel a bit anxious. I also sing in tongues.

What is the conclusion then? ***I will pray with the spirit****, and I will also pray with the understanding.* ***I will sing with the spirit****, and I will also sing with the understanding.*
— *I Corinthians 14:15*

Notice that Paul says, "I will pray with my spirit." It's an act of the will. Once you have been Baptized in the Holy Spirit and receive your prayer language, you can choose to activate your prayer language anytime you want to. You can pray in the Spirit all day long if you like. You can have as much of God as you desire. You can have as much refreshing as you like. You can be filled with as much love as you can endure.

It's really difficult to hold on to hatred, malice, bitterness, and unforgiveness while praying in the Holy Spirit. Slowly the Holy Spirit starts to change your heart. As you are praying, you don't feel vulnerable or afraid; you start to feel secure in God's love and protection as you are building up your faith!

Could the Word of God be true? Can I pray through to love and peace? YES!!! If I could just get Spirit-filled Christians to use their prayer language more often, we would see miracles. Go to a prayer meeting where they allow you to pray in tongues for an hour. Build up your endurance in *praying through* to the love of God. Once you experience a victory in prayer, you will forever know what it takes to get that peace of mind again.

> *The earnest (heartfelt, continued) prayer of a righteous man makes tremendous power available [dynamic in its working].*
> *– James 5:16b AMPC*

Listen to me, if you want to exercise consistently and with more focus, you need to get into the exercise atmosphere at a gym. If you want to grow in your prayer life, start going regularly to Spirit-filled prayer meetings.

If you already have a prayer language and would like to commit to using it more, then please say this prayer with me:

Dear God,
Help me to be instant in prayer. I choose to pray in the Spirit more. No longer will I put up with an anxious spirit. I will pray in tongues to myself and God. My spirit will pray mysteries to God. Whenever I feel unhealthy malice toward anyone, I will pray in tongues. I commit myself to go deeper in my prayer life. I submit to Your leading, Holy Spirit.
Thank You in advance for the victory.
In Jesus' name, Amen

Accessing God's Love

> *For he who speaks in a tongue does not speak to men but to God, for no one understands him; however, in the spirit he speaks mysteries.*
> *– I Corinthians 14:2*

If you are not yet baptized in the Holy Spirit, I hope this has stirred you to seek it out. If you would like to receive it now, you can. John the Baptist said that it is Jesus that baptizes with the Holy Spirit.

> *I indeed baptize you with water unto repentance, but He who is coming after me is mightier than I, whose sandals I am not worthy to carry. He will baptize you with the Holy Spirit and fire.*
> *– Matthew 3:11*

> *If you then, being evil, know how to give good gifts to your children, how much more will your Father who is in heaven **give good things to those who ask Him**!*
> *– Matthew 7:11*

All you have to do is simply ask, and then by faith, begin to speak out loud the syllables that God impresses upon your heart. Please pray this simple prayer:

Dear Jesus,
I ask that You fill me with your Holy Spirit now. Baptize me today. I now, by faith, will partner with You to pray in a heavenly language.

> *And they were all filled with the Holy Spirit and began to speak with other tongues, as the Spirit gave them utterance.*
> *– Acts 2:4*

Day 14

Mercy and Truth

*³Let not **mercy and truth** forsake you; Bind them around your neck, write them on the tablet of your heart, ⁴and so find favor and high esteem in the sight of God and man.*
— *Proverbs 3:3-4*

Often in the Bible you will find mercy and truth coupled together. Truth must be tempered with love and mercy or it will be cold and abrasive. A few platitudes about truth come to mind:

- "It's the cold hard truth"
- "It's an inconvenient truth"
- "The truth is hard to swallow"

If you speak the truth with love, it will soften the hard blow of reality and then, hopefully, the truth will be received. A spoonful of sugar helps the medicine go down.

Have you ever had someone tell you something completely rude, although true, and then follow it up with, "I call it like I see it"? If you want God's supernatural favor, you must make sure your motive is love. Ask yourself if what you share is beneficial and in everyone's best interest? Will this build up or beat up?

When I was a new "born-again" Christian in the 1980s, there were self-appointed prophets who were harsh and, frankly, mean. They thought this was how a "prophet" was supposed to act. To them, the office of "prophet" meant that you had a license to be brutal to the body of Christ (see Ephesians 4:11-12). There are five ministry gifts, and among them is the office of prophet. Thank God that the Prophets today have matured in their calling. A prophet can still call out sin, but his main job is to call out a person's destiny, to see obstacles and help believers overcome. Prophets and preachers are to encourage Christians to walk in truth, but in a way that builds and comforts.

> *But he who prophesies speaks edification*
> *and exhortation and comfort to men.*
> *— I Corinthians 14:3*

> *Instead, we will **speak the truth in love**, growing in every way more*
> *and more like Christ, who is the head of his body, the church.*
> *— Ephesians 4:15*

What does it look like to speak the truth in love? First of all, we need to do it prayerfully. There may be a right timing and approach. Some people need the truth straight up. They will only respect a fearless, honest assessment. I've also encountered some extremely hard-hearted individuals that needed the truth presented like a slap in the face. The same approach does not work with everyone's situation. Some very tender-hearted people need a softer approach. There can even be times when you are not permitted to share something with someone; the Holy Spirit wants to speak to them first before He sends prophets. The bottom line is our ultimate motivation; do we honestly have the best interest of others at heart? Love will find the best way.

> *[1]Brethren, if a man is overtaken in any trespass, you who*
> *are spiritual restore such a one in a spirit of gentleness,*
> *considering yourself lest you also be tempted. [2]Bear one*
> *another's burdens, and so fulfill the law of Christ.*
> *— Galatians 6:1-2*

This Bible verse tells us that it's our responsibility to stage an intervention if we are spiritual and truly love someone who is stumbling. Notice the attitude we are to have in our approach, "considering yourself lest you also be tempted." This is not the attitude of arrogance, but humility. May the Lord help us to speak the truth in love. Never apologize for the truth of God's Word. No matter how you dip the truth in golden honey, it can still offend someone. Just because there

Supernatural Love

is a risk that someone may not receive the truth, that doesn't alleviate your responsibility to share it. You and I are accountable to God for our action, not the reaction. To say nothing when God tells you to give a divine warning is to share in their sins.

Pray with me:

Dear Heavenly Father,
I want to couple truth with mercy. Help me to find the balance.
I don't want to be too harsh, nor do I want to ignore sin. Please
give me the wisdom to know when and how to share truth. Let
my motivation always be love. I ask that You infuse me with Your
powerful supernatural love to speak the truth today.
In Jesus' name, Amen

Tough Love

God's love for us is expressed in many wonderful ways.
One important way His love is expressed
is in loving chastisement, or discipline.
~ Alan Leonhardt

Day 15

Loving Discipline

> *⁵And you have forgotten the exhortation which speaks to you as to sons: "My son, do not despise the chastening of the Lord, Nor be discouraged when you are **rebuked** by Him; ⁶For whom the Lord loves He **chastens**, and **scourges** every son whom He receives."*
> *– Hebrews 12:5-6*

God's love for us is expressed in many wonderful ways. One important way His love is expressed is in loving chastisement, or discipline. God is not the great enabler in the sky. He is not like your parents who doted on you and gave in to your every demand whenever you threw a hissy fit. He doesn't give participation awards. He is also not an abusive parent. He is the perfect parent.

Notice the three words I emboldened in the above Bible verses: *chastens*, *rebuked*, and *scourges*. By looking at the Greek words and their meaning, we can see three stages of loving discipline.

- **Chasten** (Greek, paideia) meaning "to instruct". When you train a child, you start by instructing them on right and wrong behavior. You can't punish a child for doing wrong until he or she knows what is wrong, i.e., "Don't touch the stove."
- **Rebuke** (Greek, elegcho) meaning to verbally reprove. "Now I told you not to touch that stove. If you try and touch it again, I will have to punish you."
- **Scourge** (Greek, mastigoo) meaning to flog, or whip. God is not a child abuser, but He will spank. The concept of corporal punishment is in the Bible. Young children may not know how to talk clearly, but they understand a stinging

switch across their little behinds. A temporary sting is not abusive to a child. Never discipline a child while you're angry. Count to ten and cool off, then calmly get up and whack their buttocks. There must be reward for good behavior, and negative consequences for bad behavior, or else we won't learn.

> *He who spares his rod hates his son, but he who loves him disciplines him promptly.*
> *– Proverbs 13:24*

> *Foolishness is bound up in the heart of a child;*
> *The rod of correction will drive it far from him.*
> *– Proverbs 22:15*

> *[13] Do not withhold correction from a child, for if you beat him with a rod, he will not die.*
> *[14] You shall beat him with a rod, and deliver his soul from hell.*
> *– Proverbs 23:13-14*

    I want to make it clear that the Bible is not speaking about physical abuse. It's talking about loving discipline from emotionally stable caregivers. Some folks have come from abusive homes and don't believe in corporal punishment for small children. I understand their concern, but we are not going to change or compromise the wisdom of the Bible because of abusers. When a child grows out of the infant stage, other forms of disciple can be effective; taking something away, sitting in a time-out, etc..

    One of the ways that my Heavenly Father scourges me is through conviction. I feel so bad about my disobedience that I sulk for a day. Another way that God disciplines me is by letting others see what a fool I am and letting me suffer a little embarrassment. God is not shaming me; I have embarrassed myself by my foolish action.

    Final thoughts: God loves us. He knows that left unchecked, we will hurt ourselves and others. He would not be a loving Father if He did not correct us.

> *Now no chastening seems to be joyful for the present, but painful; nevertheless, afterward it yields the peaceable fruit of righteousness to those who have been trained by it.*
> *— Hebrews 12:11*

Dear Heavenly Father,
Help me to receive Your correction, which is for my good. Give me discernment to recognize Your chastisement when it comes. I want to be trained. I want to grow into maturity. I want to please You. In Jesus' name, Amen

Day 16

As Many as I Love, I Rebuke

*As many as I love, I rebuke and chasten.
Therefore be zealous and repent.*
— Revelation 3:19

The person who said this is none other than Jesus. Yep, that's right, loving Jesus. Love is not always expressed in positive affirmations. If I love someone, I'm going to encourage them to do the right thing.

*Faithful are the wounds of a friend,
But the kisses of an enemy are deceitful.*
— Proverbs 27:6

It's an enemy that flatters you and lies to you. A true and good friend will love you enough to confront you with a hard truth. It may be something that you don't want to hear. It may hurt you to hear it, but you need to hear it. A good friend does not want to see a greater hurt and pain come to your life. Do you have a friend that loves you enough to tell you the truth? Even when you don't want to hear it?

It's a good thing to encourage and build people up by complimenting their best qualities, however, it becomes flattery when a person's compliments are excessive. A sweet-talking flatterer is setting you up to ultimately take advantage of you in some way.

*He who rebukes a man will find more favor afterward
than he who flatters with the tongue.*
— Proverbs 28:23

Supernatural Love

> *¹Help, Lord, for the godly man ceases! For the faithful disappear from among the sons of men. ²They speak idly everyone with his neighbor; With flattering lips and a double heart they speak.*
> *– Psalms 12:1-2*

Preachers can be guilty of holding back hard truths because they don't want to offend. They want to grow a church and fill up the pews. Some preachers are stingy about giving a strong challenging word. Personally, I love to be challenged. I don't want to submit to someone's angry rant, but to be lovingly challenged by a sincere heart is precious.

> *And Joses, who was also named Barnabas by the apostles (which is translated Son of Encouragement), a Levite of the country of Cyprus.*
> *– Acts 4:36*

Here we have a man in the early church who had an amazing gift of exhortation, or encouragement. The apostles gave him a new name, Barnabas, which meant "son of encouragement." When a revival broke out at Antioch, the elders of the Jerusalem church sent Barnabas to encourage the new believers in their newfound faith.

> *²²Then news of these things came to the ears of the church in Jerusalem, and they sent out Barnabas to go as far as Antioch. ²³When he came and had seen the grace of God, he was glad, and* **encouraged them all that with purpose of heart they should continue with the Lord.** *²⁴For he was a good man, full of the Holy Spirit and of faith. And a great many people were added to the Lord.*
> *– Acts 11:22-24*

Notice how Holy Spirit-led encouragement is different from flattery. A person with a gift of exhortation will encourage people to do right and seek the Lord. A flatterer will affirm people no matter how they live.

There was a reality show named American Idol that was very popular in its first few seasons. I watched a couple of seasons with my daughters, who were teenagers at that time. Every season the show spotlighted some poor self-deceived soul who believed that he/she could sing. The star wannabe always had a small entourage of flattering followers. They

Tough Love

would affirm the singer in his/her fantasy of awesomeness. The singer would perform before the panel of judges and would crash and burn in spectacular failure. One judge would sarcastically say, "Don't quit your day job." As the morbid entertainment continued, the flattering friends would continue to encourage the person, who sounded like a strangled cat, that he/she had amazing singing talent.

What is true love? Is it always telling people just what they want to hear, or is it lovingly telling people what they NEED to hear?

As many as I love, I rebuke and chasten.
Therefore be zealous and repent.
— Revelation 3:19

Dear Heavenly Father,
Help me to give the right kind of encouragement at the right time. I want to build people up in righteousness, not self-deception. If there are people who need to hear the truth, please give me the courage to speak the truth in love. Help me to love people into the way of righteousness.
In Jesus' name, Amen

Day 17

Don't Be Unequally Yoked

*Do not be unequally yoked together with unbelievers.
For what fellowship has righteousness with lawlessness?
And what communion has light with darkness?*
— II Corinthians 6:14

Every Christian I know wants to see people get saved and set free from the penalty of sin. I, too, want to display God's love and make serving God as appealing as possible. I want to be like Jesus, be the friend of sinners, and love people into the Kingdom (see Luke 7:34). But how can I be a friend of sinners and obey the above scripture? At what point am I unequally yoked together with an unbeliever? Being unequally yoked with unbelievers means more than having bad business partners, or missionary dating, it's about having toxic friendships as well.

You may be asking, "What does this have to do with loving people?" Being a loving person does not mean that you let people drag you down. Part of loving others is being strong for people who truly need and WANT your help. You can't help someone unless they want it. This is more about how to lovingly walk away when you are unequally yoked with an unbeliever, or someone claiming to be a believer who is actually living for themselves.

When I was a Youth Pastor, I helped my students balance this out by posing these thoughts to them, "How do you know when you are unequally yoked together with unbelievers? It's when they are having more of a negative influence on you than you are influencing them for the Lord. Who is influencing who? If a relationship is toxic, don't make yourself so available. You may have to immediately cut off all ties."

You are not indestructible. You have to protect yourself and your relationship with God. Appropriate boundaries need to be put in place. It's good to want to love people and see them saved, but if you have just been delivered from alcoholism, you should not be hanging around bars and drinking parties. You must get strong in the Lord so that your vulnerabilities are protected and strengthened. When an airplane flight begins, the flight attendant gives a presentation on how to put on the oxygen mask. They advise you that if you have small children, you put the mask on yourself first before you help your children with theirs. This is because if something happens to you, there would be no one to help and take care of your children. It's important that you get healthy and strong before you launch out into dark places.

If you feel tempted to compromise when you are with certain people, then you should not make yourself available to hang out with them. This gets tricky when you have unsaved lifelong friends, and now you have been radically saved. They want to go out and party, but you want to go to a worship service. As hard as it may sound, you may have to start distancing yourself from those relationships. There are sacrifices in serving Jesus; you do have to give up certain things to serve Christ. Ask yourself the tough questions: Who is influencing who? Are they open to your new life in Christ? Will they come to church with you? Don't follow them back into your old life.

I was a popular person with the party crowd before I was born again. The change in my life was so abrupt, and I did such a radical 180-degree turn, that many thought I had lost my mind. One night some friends came to pick me up to go to a revelry of booze and drugs, and I brought my Bible into the car. One friend asked, "Why are you bringing that Bible?", to which I responded, "Didn't you say this was a BYOB party? Bring Your Own Bible?" My friends didn't think my joke was as humorous as I did.

We are attracted to people like us; people who share the same values and have the same worldview. Most of the time we are friends with people around our age who share the same stage of life. High School students are friends. College students are friends. Young married couples with children are friends. Retired folks with grandchildren are friends, and so forth. You can tell a lot about people by their friendships with others. Birds of a feather DO flock together. A Christian should have a desire to fellowship with other believers. They should want to have friends they can pray with, and talk about God and His Word. If someone claims to be a Christian but avoids other Spirit-filled Christians, something is wrong.

You can be friends with unbelievers and influence them for Christ, but you should have Christian friends as well. Love is not partaking in the same sins as your unsaved friends. How is *that* a good witness for the Lord? Love is displaying the hope of a changed life. People deep down want to see you succeed in your walk with God. They want to know that there is an option available to them when they are ready to change. Keep offering that hope.

> *So stop fooling yourselves! Evil companions will corrupt good morals and character.*
> *– I Corinthians 15:33*

> *If you want to grow in wisdom, spend time with the wise.*
> *Walk with the wicked and you'll eventually become just like them.*
> *– Proverbs 13:20*

> *(Love) does not rejoice in iniquity, but rejoices in the truth.*
> *– I Corinthians 13:6*

Dear God,
Help me to have Your discernment. Speak to me about my friendships. If it's time for me to move on, please show me. Holy Spirit, give me a consistent witness in my spirit. Surround me with wise counselors who know You and Your ways. If I have friends that You don't want me to give up on, please help me to be a good witness to them.
In Jesus' name I pray, Amen

Day 18

Love is Discerning

⁹And this I pray, that your love may abound still more and more in knowledge and all discernment, ¹⁰that you may approve the things that are excellent, that you may be sincere and without offense till the day of Christ.
– Philippians 1:9-10

Have you ever been manipulated? Some people will tell you that you're not a loving Christian unless you agree with their outrageous lifestyle. They will put a guilt trip on you and call you judgmental because you dare to discern something to be a sin. I just want to set the record straight; I can love others and not agree with their lifestyle.

Did you know that in Canada it's a hate crime for a minister to teach that homosexuality is a sin? In the United States it's not against the law to teach that homosexuality is a sin, but many in the church will treat you like you committed a hate crime. Do I have the right as a Christian to judge homosexuality as a sin that will send a person to Hell? Stating it like that makes discerning sin sound pretty harsh.

To discern something is to distinguish, discriminate, and judge. The Bible develops antithetical thinking. It is constantly making distinctions between good and evil, right and wrong, clean and unclean. The kind of judgment that is wrong is when we condemn. Only God can condemn. We are to *discern*.

Even a child is known by his deeds, whether what he does is pure and right.
– Proverbs 20:11

Okay, I brought up the whole "homosexuality" issue. Let's look at just two New Testament verses that teach homosexuality is a sin.

> ^{26}*For this reason God gave them up to vile passions. For even their women exchanged the natural use for what is against nature.* ^{27}*Likewise also the men, leaving the natural use of the woman, burned in their lust for one another, men with men committing what is shameful, and receiving in themselves the penalty of their error which was due.*
> *— Romans 1:26-27*

> ^{9}*Do you not know that* **the unrighteous will not inherit the kingdom of God***? Do not be deceived. Neither fornicators, nor idolaters,* **nor adulterers, nor homosexuals, nor sodomites***,* ^{10}*nor thieves, nor covetous, nor drunkards, nor revilers, nor extortioners will inherit the kingdom of God.*
> *— I Corinthians 6:9-10*

These verses not only condemn homosexuality as sin, but they also state that a person who lives a lifestyle of sexual sin will NOT go to heaven. The good news is that a person can turn to God, repent, and be washed clean from sin.

> *And such* ***were*** *some of you. But you were washed, but you were sanctified, but you were justified in the name of the Lord Jesus and by the Spirit of our God*
> *— I Corinthians 6:11*

How can I know something is wrong and destructive if I cannot discern by the Word of God? That's what growing in your faith is all about; it's about growing closer to God and learning what pleases Him.

If I come across a bridge that is washed away by a flood, and discern that anyone who drives down this road will careen into raging waters and ultimately drown, and I do nothing… how is that love? If I don't warn homosexuals, and all sinners for that matter, that their lifestyle will destroy them, am I a loving person if I affirm them as "okay?" If I truly love someone, I will want to try to rescue them from self-deception and self-destruction.

Tough Love

Dear heavenly Father,
Help my love to grow in knowledge and discernment. Give me the strength to make distinctions about what is sin without hating the sinner. Love does not rejoice in iniquity, but rejoices in the truth (see I Corinthians 13:6). Teach me how to encourage people in righteousness.
In Jesus' name, Amen

Day 19

Romantic Love

Guard your heart above all else, for it determines the course of your life.
— Proverbs 4:23 NLT

I charge you, O daughters of Jerusalem, By the gazelles or by the does of the field, do not stir up nor awaken love Until it pleases.
— Song of Solomon 2:7

Let's do some myth-busting. Romantic love has so many misconceptions and deceptions around it that it's no wonder people have unmet expectations. Let's use the Christmas holiday season as an example. Every year there is such a build-up for Christmas; television specials that leave us with warm fuzzy feelings and always have a happy ending, and the commercial drive to find happiness in gifts, family, and romance. It's no wonder people experience such a letdown on Christmas morning. It can be like post-birth depression. Sadly, suicide rates are the highest around the Christmas holidays.

Now before you think I'm a Scrooge, I love the Christmas season. I have great memories of wonderful past Christmases. But then again, I'm an eternal optimist; a glass-half-full kind of guy. I can make a dying-of-thirst experience in the desert seem like great alone-time; an opportunity to fast, enjoy God, and the stillness of nature.

I also want you to know that I believe romantic love exists. The Song of Solomon is an eternal testimony that burning passion and romantic love between a man and a woman is real and okay with God. Romantic love is not a myth; the myths I am referring to are several unrealistic and deceptive views of romantic love that could lead to destruction. Because this is a devotional, I am only addressing the #1 myth that destroys marriages and lives.

#1 MYTH: FALLING IN LOVE

Before you tune me out, please consider some things. While it is true that sometimes close friendships can deepen to something more, the idea that you have no control over whom you fall in love with is a myth. When people say that you can't choose whom you fall in love with, the hairs on the back of my neck stand up. That's spooky and deceptive. There is infatuation, attraction, and chemistry, but ultimately you are in control of your feelings. You are not a slave to your feelings and thoughts. As a born-again spiritual being, you are to cast down feelings and thoughts contrary to the Word of God and the will of God.

> *⁴For the weapons of our warfare are not carnal but mighty in God for pulling down strongholds, ⁵casting down arguments and every high thing that exalts itself against the knowledge of God, bringing every thought into captivity to the obedience of Christ.*
> *– II Corinthians 10:4-5*

As a spiritual being, you have the Spirit of the living God dwelling inside of you. Random thoughts and emotions don't have to dominate you. You are to *rule over them*. God never commands us to do something without imparting the power to carry it out. He tells you not to be unequally yoked together with unbelievers (see II Corinthians 6:14-16). So, if you have no control over with whom you "fall in love", then you have no choice in marrying an unbeliever. You could randomly fall in love with a Buddhist, a 90-year-old person, or someone of the same sex. This frustrates the Word of God. When the Bible tells you to crucify the flesh, this is what it means. When desires arise that are contrary to the Word of God, you must overcome them and put them to death (see Ephesians 4:17-24).

> *And those who are Christ's have **crucified the flesh** with its passions and desires.*
> *– Galatians 5:24*

Supernatural Love

I know that this line of thinking goes against all modern cultures. It goes against years of propaganda from songs and movies that we have seen and listened to over the years. But think about it, if you have no control over whom you "fall in love" with, then you can just as easily "fall out of love." That means that a marriage covenant is subject to the whims of your moods. This means that your relationship with God is also subject to your feelings. Today you may feel saved, but then tomorrow you don't. Think about the phrase, "crucified the flesh." The death penalty of crucifixion was a long and excruciatingly painful process. There are times in this life when you must put to death feelings that are pulling you out of the will of God. No one said it was easy. What makes it hard and painful at times is our sinful nature; the flesh. God will give you the grace (divine empowerment) to overcome. If you have ever had strong feelings for someone, and then God told you to break it off, you understand what it means to crucify the flesh.

Romantic love in the confines of God's will and blessing is a profoundly wonderful thing. You will know love beyond superficial feelings and surface infatuation. You can know romantic love that is emotional and spiritual. The depth of this kind of love can only be found with God at the center. When both people in a relationship love God and have placed Him as their first priority, then as they grow closer to the Lord, they will also grow closer to each other.

Guard your heart above all else, for it determines the course of your life.
– Proverbs 4:23 NLT

Put a sentinel on your heart; don't awaken love out of God's timing. Your heart is not a cheap and trivial thing that you can freely scatter around at a whim. Your heart is a great gift for the right person. As you seek God first, He will arrange the proper time for you to run right into your true love and life companion.

But seek first the kingdom of God and His righteousness,
and all these things shall be added to you.
– Matthew 6:33

Tough Love

Dear Heavenly Father,
I want to know true love. Please keep me from being led astray by my feelings. I look to You to awaken love in its proper time and with the proper person.
In Jesus' name, Amen

Day 20

Love and Marriage

Nevertheless let each one of you in particular so love his own wife as himself, and let the wife see that she respects her husband.
– Ephesians 5:33

I decide what kind of marriage I will have. I can choose to make my life a hell on earth, or relatively wonderful. It all starts and ends with my attitude. If I treat my wife with respect, patience, and understanding, then my wife will treat me the same way. There are always exceptions to the rule, whereas no matter how much you give into your marriage relationship, it is not reciprocated. Generally, it holds true that you get what you give. It's the Golden rule: "Treat others the way you would like to be treated." It's the law of sowing and reaping: "Whatever a man sows, that he will also reap" (see Galatians 6:7).

Never take each other for granted by taking out the stresses of life on one another. Your spouse is not your whipping post whenever you get frustrated at work. It's not the responsibility of your spouse to bring you ultimate happiness and fulfillment. Only God can do that. If you are dissatisfied with life, don't blame your spouse; seek God about some faith goals, and then make a change.

I can't give you twenty steps to a fulfilling marriage in one devotional, but I can give you the ultimate element that will make a marriage great and lasting: **Treat each other with respect.** When you get frustrated and yell, apologize. Don't make big money decisions without being in unity. Sacrifice hobbies and time for one another. Compliment often. Say "I love you" several times a day.

Tough Love

It was an ancient African custom when proposing to a young woman to give the father a cow, or cows. It was very rare for a bride to be valued at ten cows. It was rumored that a rich prince was coming to the village to choose a bride. All of the eligible young women made themselves look their best and lined up as the prince walked through the village.

At the outskirts of town lived a very poor family. The father was disabled from a farming accident and the house became a shack. The daughter was constantly picked on by the other young women because she dressed in rags. The poor girl didn't even bother to line up with the other girls. What was the point? She figured she would never be picked anyway.

The prince gave a casual glance at all of the young ladies as he passed through the village. Then, he stopped at the edge of town and stared at the poor girl doing her family laundry. The silence was briefly interrupted by some giggling as some of the other girls laughed at the sight. Surely the prince would say something derogatory about this disheveled girl. The prince went to the poor girl and asked her name. He then motioned to an assistant in his entourage and offered ten cows to the father to marry his daughter. The village was in shock! Even the poor girl's father tried to talk the prince out of his decision, but the prince kept insisting that she was a ten-cow woman.

Several years had gone by and the prince returned to the village with his wife. When the villagers saw the prince's beautiful wife they were outraged, "What have you done with the girl? Did you sell her to slave traders?" The prince assured them that this was the same young woman that he picked to be his bride. He said, "This is my beautiful ten-cow woman!"

This story beautifully illustrates the power of love and respect. If we believe the best and honor one another, who knows the potential that will bloom out of meager beginnings.

Whenever I am filled with self-doubt, my wife always encourages me. I am a very self-confident person, but I still love it when my wife

Supernatural Love

believes in my potential. Behind every great man is a great woman, and visa-versa.

What a paradise it would be if we lived to build each other up and looked for ways to make life easier for the ones we love. It's not too late; begin to sow love and respect. Don't wait for the other person to start. Don't stop if you feel like your efforts are not appreciated. Keep it up. You are breaking down walls. Love never fails.

> [9] *And let us not grow weary while doing good, for in due season we shall reap if we do not lose heart.* [10] *Therefore, as we have opportunity, let us do good to all, especially to those who are of the household of faith.*
> *– Galatians 6:9-10*

Dear God,
Help me to love my spouse with Godly love. I choose to speak life to my husband/wife. Give me the wisdom to know how to encourage and build up my marriage. Show me the keys to unlocking the potential in my mate. I choose the path of life. I choose to sow love and respect. If I fail, I will try again. I will not give up.
In Jesus' name, Amen

Day 21

Love One Another

³⁴A new commandment I give to you, that you love one another; as I have loved you, that you also love one another. ³⁵By this all will know that you are My disciples, if you have love for one another.
— John 13:34-35

So many times the New Testament tells us to love one another, forgive one another, and have patience with one another. In the above scripture, it is a sign that we are true disciples of Christ. When we are submitted to the Holy Spirit, we will obey this command.

When we are in the flesh and obeying our sinful nature, we will experience pride, strife, and division. There will be divisive people in the body of Christ who, no matter how much you love them, cause trouble. Some are wolves in sheep's clothing. For sure we need to be on the side of love, but what if I am for peace and they are always for war?

⁵Woe is me, that I dwell in Meshech, That I dwell among the tents of Kedar! ⁶My soul has dwelt too long with one who hates peace.
⁷I am for peace; But when I speak, they are for war.
— Psalms 120:5-7

The people of Meshech and Kedar were nomadic people, always at war. They were wild and brutal. Their hand was against every man, and every man's hand was against them. Some of their relatives are still alive today, always looking for a fight. They don't know how to live with others in peace. It's also a terrible witness to the world when people in the church are fighting.

Some people are like a wounded beat-up dog. They have trust issues because they come from abusive situations. With proper loving care and patience, God can heal them. Some rebellious scoundrels feign that they're wounded in order to take advantage of the mercy-motivated among us. Evil exists, and predators lurk around the watering hole looking to isolate their prey. Loving the people of God is to protect them from demonized reprobates. A true pastor has an anointing to drive out predators. We need discernment from the Holy Spirit.

> [34] *But David said to Saul, "Your servant used to keep his father's sheep, and when a lion or a bear came and took a lamb out of the flock,* [35] *I went out after it and struck it, and delivered the lamb from its mouth; and when it arose against me, I caught it by its beard, and struck and killed it."*
> – I Samuel 17:34-35

RIGHTEOUS DIVISION

The church is so messed up, we want to love the predators and bash the people protecting us. This may be an inconvenient truth but Jesus came to bring division; a righteous division. Sure, He came to seek and to save the lost, to give life more abundantly, and to destroy the works of the devil. But He also came to bring division.

> [34] *Do not think that I came to bring peace on earth. I did not come to bring peace but a sword...* [36] *and a man's enemies will be those of his own household.*
> – Matthew 10:34,36

> *For there must also be factions among you, that those who are approved may be recognized among you.*
> – I Corinthians 11:19

Truth *will* divide. It can even divide families. To be a loving person is to love the truth. Lies will destroy people we love. But the paradox of Christian love is that your love for the truth will not always be seen as love for others. Preaching some of the truths of the Bible is considered hate crimes in many countries. The side of love is always the side of truth. But that truth is not overbearing; we do not bully others into believing in truth. We speak the truth with love.

UNRIGHTEOUS DIVISION

> *[1]And I, brethren, could not speak to you as to **spiritual** people but as to **carnal**, as to **babes in Christ**. [2]I fed you with milk and not with solid food; for until now you were not able to receive it, and even now you are still not able; [3]for **you are still carnal. For where there are envy, strife, and divisions among you, are you not carnal and behaving like mere men?***
> *– I Corinthians 3:1-3*

In the above passages, there are three different groups of Christians; Spiritual, carnal, and babes in Christ. The carnal Christian is not divisive because he loves the truth, he is divisive because he is contentious, envious, and prideful. There is a difference between divisions brought on because of obedience and love of the truth, and those brought on by carnal Christians. If you are being contentious with others in your local church, it's very important that you examine your heart. Confess your sin of sowing discord among brothers, and turn from your sin before a sudden calamity befalls you.

> *[12]A worthless person, a wicked man, Walks with a perverse mouth; [13]He winks with his eyes, He shuffles his feet, He points with his fingers; [14]Perversity is in his heart, He devises evil continually,* ***He sows discord.*** *[15]**Therefore his calamity shall come suddenly; suddenly he shall be broken without remedy.***
> *– Proverbs 6:12-15*

The seventh abomination, in Proverbs 6:19, is one who sows discord among brethren.

There is a renewal from heaven that brings us into unity. When a church is in unity, there is love. Love brings about unity, and unity brings about love. In ourselves, we cannot love the way God wants us to love. We need the power of the Holy Spirit to earnestly and fervently love one another in truth, not in hypocritical pretense.

Supernatural Love

Have you ever been to a fund-raising dinner where people put on fake smiles and the room is filled with forced laughter? Outwardly, they appear to care, but inwardly they are ravenous wolves full of dead men's bones. The whole fund-raising dinner seems to say, "We want your money, but we don't really give a rip about you."

I want my love to be sincere. I love others because God commands me to. I obey His command to love by faith and eventually my feelings follow. I love others because I am loved by God. Because God values and loves me, I can love myself and others. I love others because I want to be a good witness to the world. *"By this all will know that you are My disciples, if you have love for one another" John 13:35.*

> *Since you have purified your souls in obeying the truth through the Spirit in **sincere love of the brethren**, love one another fervently with a pure heart.*
> *– I Peter 1:22*

Epilogue

I trust that this devotional has enriched and expanded your understanding of God's supernatural love. Let us lay hold of a love that is beyond human effort. Let's cry out to the Lord for a compassion for our fellow man; a compassion for the lost; a compassion for the dregs of humanity; and a compassion for the feeble and infirm.

Jesus said that in the last days the love of many would grow cold. I prophesy to these dry bones, *"Live! Let the four winds blow the breath of life into you. I command fervent love to burn fresh in your heart and spirit now! In the mighty name of Jesus. Amen"*

Supernatural Love

www.ingramcontent.com/pod-product-compliance
Lightning Source LLC
Chambersburg PA
CBHW071913070526
44583CB00016B/1975